STORM WARNING

STORM WARNING

TORNADOES AND HURRICANES

by Jonathan D. Kahl

Lerner Publications Company / Minneapolis

For Joey and Carol

Words printed in **bold** are explained in the glossary that begins on page 59.

A metric conversion chart appears on page 61.

Library of Congress Cataloging-in-Publication Data

Kahl, Jonathan D.
    Storm warning: tornadoes and hurricanes / Jonathan D. Kahl.
      p.   cm.—(How's the weather?)
    Includes index.
    Summary: Provides information about hurricanes and tornadoes, such as where and when they occur, how they form, and the damage they can cause.
    ISBN 0-8225-2527-5
    1. Tornadoes—Juvenile literature. 2. Hurricanes—Juvenile literature.
[1. Tornadoes. 2. Hurricanes.] I. Title. II. Series: Kahl, Jonathan D. How's the weather?
QC955.K34 1993   92-13627
551.55'3—dc20   CIP
                                          AC

Manufactured in the United States of America

1 2 3 4 5 6 98 97 96 95 94 93

CONTENTS

INTRODUCTION

Can you imagine winds of more than 150 miles per hour that uproot trees and toss train cars through the air? Think about massive floods caused by two feet of rain falling in a single day. If you have ever been in the path of a **tornado** or **hurricane**, you might have experienced such devastation firsthand. Few weather events are more spectacular or more destructive than tornadoes and hurricanes, the most violent storms on Earth.

Many people are interested in tornadoes and hurricanes—and just about everybody is afraid of them. People who live in the tornado-prone areas of the central United States, for example, take shelter in basements and storm cellars when a tornado is spotted. Residents of coastal cities along the Atlantic Ocean and the Gulf of Mexico keep plenty of wood, hammers, and nails handy to board up their windows during hurricane season.

Meteorologists, the scientists who study and predict the weather, find tornadoes and hurricanes intriguing for several reasons. First, meteorologists have a difficult time predicting where and when tornadoes and hurricanes will form. Scientists are also puzzled about

This small plane was flipped by a twister.

how tornadoes and hurricanes can unleash extraordinary amounts of energy in certain places, while leaving surrounding areas quiet and calm.

In this book, you will learn where and when tornadoes and hurricanes occur, how they form, the damage they can cause, and how they affect people. You'll find out how meteorologists predict tornadoes and hurricanes, and you'll read fascinating accounts of famous tornadoes and hurricanes. Let's try to unravel the mysteries of the most ferocious and terrifying storms on Earth.

1

TORNADO WEATHER

A tornado, sometimes called a "cyclone" or a "twister," is a fierce, swirling wind that takes the shape of a funnel. Tornadoes form during severe **thunderstorms.** So, places that receive a lot of thunderstorms are also likely to have tornadoes. Although tornadoes have been reported in all parts of the world—except in extremely cold regions—most tornadoes occur in the United States. In fact, more than 600 tornadoes touch down in the United States every year.

Tornadoes are most common in the "Tornado Alley" area of the United States, which stretches from Texas to Iowa. This region receives just the right balance of sunshine, wind, and **humidity** (the amount of moisture in the air) needed for thunderstorms to form. One of the Tornado Belt states is Kansas, the scene of the famous twister that whisked Dorothy off to a magical land over the rainbow in the classic story *The Wizard of Oz*.

Most tornadoes (and thunderstorms) occur during the spring and early summer months—between March and July. Tornadoes sometimes form during other seasons, but winter tornadoes are extremely rare. Tornadoes usually occur in the late afternoon, just

A funnel cloud races through farmland.

after temperatures have reached their highest levels for the day. When dealing with tornadoes, however, we can't take anything for granted. These deadly storms have been known to form at any time of the day or night. They have been reported as far north as Alaska and as far south as Australia.

Since tornadoes form inside thunderstorms, we'll need to take a closer look at thunderstorms. The word "thunderstorm" refers not only to a turbulent, short-lived rainstorm but also to the kind of *cloud* that causes such a storm. Another name for a thunderstorm is a **cumulonimbus cloud**.

An electrical storm lights up the night sky.

Thunderstorms are giant clouds. A thunderstorm might grow to an altitude, or height, of six or seven miles. The cloud might be more than a mile wide at its base. Sometimes thunderstorms form in clusters or lines that can stretch for 60 miles or more. A typical thunderstorm contains enough water to fill an Olympic-size swimming pool.

A thunderstorm is pretty exciting all by itself—even without a tornado. Thunderstorms generate thunder and lightning as well as rain. A thunderstorm can create strong gusting winds and balls of ice called hailstones. Late afternoon thunderstorms are sometimes followed by rainbows, a colorful reward to those who have been inconvenienced by the rain.

THE ATMOSPHERE

The atmosphere is the blanket of air surrounding the Earth. In the troposphere, the lowest layer of the atmosphere, air becomes colder the higher up you go. Temperatures are low at high altitudes because most of the Sun's heat passes through the troposphere without heating it at all. Instead, the Sun's heat goes straight to the land and oceans, warming them up.

The Earth holds the heat and slowly warms the air above it. As a result, the warmest part of the troposphere is closest to the ground. Even on a hot summer day, the air at the top of a tall mountain, or at the top of a thunderstorm, can be frigid!

Cloud Formation

A thunderstorm, like other clouds, is made up of millions and millions of tiny drops of water and tiny ice crystals floating in the air. We can see clouds, but there is a lot of water in the air that we can't see. Most of the water in the air takes the form of an invisible gas called **water vapor**. Water vapor is liquid water that has been **evaporated**—turned into a gas—by the heat of the Sun.

Clouds form by a process called **condensation**, which is the opposite of evaporation. Condensation occurs when water vapor cools and turns from gas back into liquid water. When condensation occurs, the tiny drops of water in the air form clouds.

Condensation often occurs, and clouds often form, when moist air rises to high altitudes—where temperatures are very low. There, water vapor in the air cools and condenses, forming a cloud.

Moist air rises for several reasons. One way that air rises from the ground is by heating. The rising motion of warm air is called **convection**. Another way that air rises from the ground is by **frontal lifting**. **Fronts** are boundaries created where cold air pushes into warm air (or vice versa). When warm and cold air bump into each other, the colder air sinks and the warmer air rises. A third type of rising motion, **orographic lifting**, is caused by mountains. When winds blow toward a mountain range, they rise to high altitudes along the slope of the mountains.

The three types of lifting—convective, frontal, and orographic—are responsible for the creation of many types of clouds. When water vapor condenses inside a cloud, the condensation process creates a special kind of energy called **latent heat**. As latent heat warms the air inside the cloud, the warm air rises even higher.

A thunderstorm grows near Albin, Wyoming.

LATENT HEAT

You can learn how condensation adds heat to the air by heating a pan of water on your stove. What happens to the stove's heat? At first, heat from the stove increases the temperature of the water. After several minutes, the temperature reaches the boiling point: 212° F.

Even though the stove continues to add heat to the water, the water remains at 212° F. Why? Instead of increasing the temperature of the water, the heat from the burner is now working to evaporate the water—to turn it into water vapor.

The energy that changes water into water vapor is called latent heat (*latent* means "hidden"). We can't feel latent heat, but it isn't lost—it's *hidden* inside water vapor. In turn, condensation, the opposite of evaporation, causes latent heat to "come out of hiding" so we can feel it again. The latent heat that is released as water vapor condenses warms the air inside clouds. The warm air rises higher, helping thunderstorms to grow.

Cumulus clouds look pleasant, but they can grow into violent thunderstorms.

A cloud that contains a lot of moisture will produce a lot of latent heat. The cloud will grow taller and taller—and become a towering thunderstorm.

The Thunderstorm Life Cycle

A thunderstorm goes through three distinct stages during its existence: the cumulus, mature, and dissipating stages. The entire process usually takes about two hours. The *cumulus* stage of a thunderstorm often starts on hot summer days when the air near the ground is warm and moist.

Convection lifts the moist air to higher altitudes where the air begins to cool. Water vapor in the air condenses into tiny liquid water droplets. The droplets form a **cumulus cloud**, the kind of puffy white cloud commonly seen on summer afternoons.

As the latent heat of condensation warms the air inside the cloud, the air rises higher and cools again. The cloud grows taller. (If a front or a mountain is nearby, the cloud may grow even faster.) The cumulus cloud grows into a tall cumulonimbus cloud—a thunderstorm.

The columns of rising air, or upward moving winds, inside a thunderstorm are called **updrafts**. Updrafts carry small water droplets upward through the cloud. The droplets bump into each other, combine, and grow larger and heavier. At the top of the cloud, some of the droplets freeze into tiny ice crystals. When the water droplets (and ice crystals) become too heavy to remain suspended in the air, they fall to the ground as rain. Rainfall (as well as hail, thunder, and lightning) marks the beginning of the *mature* stage of a thunderstorm.

Falling raindrops pull some air down with them, creating downward moving air currents, or **downdrafts**. As rainfall in the mature thunderstorm becomes stronger, the downdrafts grow stronger too. Before long the downdrafts become stronger than the updrafts, and the storm begins the *dissipating*, or dissolving, stage. Rainfall becomes lighter and eventually stops. Soon the mighty cumulonimbus cloud evaporates and disappears.

Thunderstorms sometimes bring hailstones along with the rain.

Tornado Formation

One feature that is noticeably absent from the thunderstorm we have just described is a tornado. Keep in mind that most thunderstorms *don't* produce tornadoes. Only the most powerful thunderstorms, *severe thunderstorms*, create tornadoes.

Severe thunderstorms form the same way that ordinary thunderstorms do—with one difference. Severe thunderstorms have strong **wind shear**. Wind shear refers to different wind conditions at different altitudes. Strong wind shear occurs when winds blowing through the upper part of a cumulonimbus cloud are more powerful and blow from a different direction than winds in the lower part of the cloud.

Imagine a pencil pointing toward the sky and floating through the air. Without wind shear, the pencil would simply move along with the wind. Now suppose a strong wind from the northwest blew toward the top of the pencil while a weak wind from the southwest blew toward the bottom of the pencil. The different winds would act together to make the pencil spin in a counterclockwise direction. Similarly, different wind conditions at different altitudes cause updrafts within a thunderstorm to rotate. With a rotating updraft, a tornado is born.

Another name for a rotating updraft is a **vortex**. Let's examine a vortex within a severe thunderstorm. Have you ever noticed how spinning ice skaters turn faster by bringing their arms in tight to their bodies? Like a spinning ice skater, a narrow vortex will rotate more quickly than a wide one. As strong updrafts and downdrafts in a thunderstorm stretch a vortex, the vortex becomes thinner and begins to rotate faster.

A vortex usually starts in the middle section of a severe thunderstorm and works its way downward. When the vortex dips below the base of the cloud, it becomes a **funnel cloud**. You might be surprised to learn that the vortex itself is invisible—because air is invisible. When we see a funnel cloud, we are really seeing water droplets swirling around with the vortex. When a funnel cloud touches down, or reaches the ground, we call it a tornado.

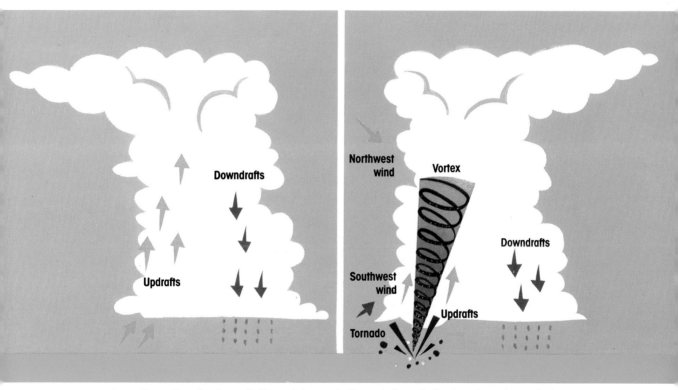

An ordinary thunderstorm (left) contains updrafts and downdrafts. In a tornado-producing thunderstorm (right), different wind conditions create wind shear. Strong wind shear causes updrafts to spin, creating a vortex.

2

TORNADOES AND PEOPLE

What are your chances of encountering a tornado during your life? Statistics tell us that the odds are against it. Less than one percent of all thunderstorms ever produce a tornado. Even in the Tornado Alley region of the central United States, an individual town is likely to be hit by a tornado only once every 250 years. There are some unusual exceptions, however. Tornadoes passed through Oklahoma City, Oklahoma, 30 times during the last 100 years alone. And May 20 is a special date for Codell, Kansas. Tornadoes passed through Codell on that day in 1916, 1917, and 1918!

Despite the slim odds, you should learn to recognize the warning signs of an approaching tornado to know whether you should move to safety. It's important to treat any severe weather with extreme caution. The same storm that brings heavy rains, strong wind gusts, and large hail may also produce a tornado.

There is no way to be absolutely sure that a severe thunderstorm will produce a tornado, but there are a few telltale signals. The first sign that a thunderstorm might produce a tornado is the appearance of **mammatus clouds**—bulging, pouchlike clouds that hang

Mammatus clouds are a warning signal that a tornado might form.

down from the base of a cumulonimbus cloud. Mammatus clouds indicate the strong updrafts and downdrafts that must be present if tornadoes are going to form.

If a portion of the base of a thunderstorm begins to rotate, there is a good chance a tornado will soon appear. First, the large rotating section, called a **wall cloud**, will start to descend toward the ground. From within the wall cloud, a smaller, more powerful vortex—the funnel cloud—will soon snake downward.

A wall cloud drops over Limon, Colorado.

The funnel touches down.

Touchdown

When a tornado touches down, the rapidly swirling vortex lifts debris, including dirt, rocks, and even trees, into the air. The debris darkens the sky (which is already quite dark because of the tall cumulonimbus cloud blocking the sunlight overhead) and adds to the menacing appearance of the tornado.

As a wall cloud drops, you might notice swirling debris before you see the funnel. Don't make the fateful mistake of assuming there's no tornado just because you can't see one. Funnel clouds can be invisible because *air* is invisible. If there are no water droplets swirling around with the air, you might not see the vortex until it begins to pick up dirt and debris. Falling rain, dust, or darkness might also block your view of a tornado.

All tornadoes are different. Nevertheless, there are some common features that many tornado observers have noticed. The sound of a nearby tornado has often been compared to the roar of a passing freight train. This noise isn't surprising, considering all the dirt, pebbles, sticks, trash, and other material clattering around within a rotating vortex. Another common observation is that the air is often calm just before a tornado hits. The noisiest and most violent areas of a thunderstorm are the sections where rain and hail are falling (the downdraft areas of the cloud). But rain doesn't fall in an updraft area of a thunderstorm. No wonder it gets quiet before a tornado.

Because a tornado is a strong, rotating updraft, tornadoes are capable of lifting large objects. Tornadoes have tossed automobiles and even railroad cars into the air, lifted the roofs off houses, and driven small pieces of wood through metal pipes. People and animals have been lifted, carried a mile or so in the air, and then been dropped back on the ground. In one bizarre incident, baby snakes rained out of the the sky over Memphis, Tennessee, in 1877. Apparently the little reptiles were sucked out of a pond into a strong cumulonimbus updraft and carried a long distance before falling to the ground.

Tornadoes not only threaten human and animal life but they also cause millions of dollars in property damage each year.

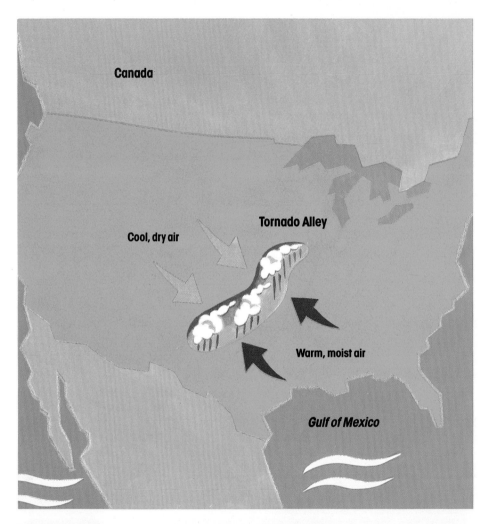

TORNADO ALLEY

Most tornadoes form in the "Tornado Alley," or "Tornado Belt," region of the central United States. In the Tornado Belt, cool, dry air flowing south from Canada often meets moist, warm air flowing north from the Gulf of Mexico. The different air currents bump into each other and form fronts. Fronts create thunderstorms, many of which are severe.

Tornado Safety

As fascinating as tornadoes are, we must never forget that the storms are quite deadly. You should never go outside when tornadoes may be nearby—especially since the severe thunderstorms that spawn tornadoes generate a lot of lightning, which can be deadly itself.

The U.S. government's National Weather Service has developed a system of "watches" and "warnings" that are used to alert the public to the dangers of severe weather. When tornadoes are likely to form but have not been spotted, the National Weather Service issues a tornado *watch*. Once a tornado has been sighted, either by a human observer or on a **radar** screen, a tornado *warning* is issued. Watches and warnings are broadcast on local television and radio stations. In some towns, warning sirens sound during severe weather.

If a tornado watch is issued for your area, stay close to a battery-operated radio or television to keep track of the danger. If the National Weather Service announces a tornado warning, or if you spot a tornado yourself, take cover immediately. According to the National Weather Service, the best places to seek shelter during a tornado are basements or strong buildings. Avoid large structures such as supermarkets and gymnasiums, which—should the roof or walls become damaged—offer little protection from falling debris. Stay away from mobile homes and cars, which a tornado can easily hurl through the air.

Most schools have a designated area where students should take shelter during a tornado—usually a hallway away from any outside walls. If you are at home during a tornado warning, go to the basement. If your house or apartment doesn't have a basement, take cover in a small room in the center of the building. Stay clear of all windows. Crouch or lie down—if possible, under a strong piece of furniture—and cover your head. Keep a battery-operated radio or television on hand to find out when the danger has passed.

If you are outdoors when a tornado is approaching, don't try to escape from the storm in a car. Tornadoes are unpredictable and move quickly. If you can't get indoors, abandon your car and lie flat in a low-lying area or an open ditch.

Studying Tornadoes

Tornadoes are generally between 300 and 1,800 feet wide at ground level. Occasionally, however, very small (10-foot wide) and very large (1-mile wide) tornadoes are reported. In addition to the spinning motion of the vortex, tornadoes move across the land— usually at speeds ranging from 25 to 45 miles per hour. Every so often, however, a twister is clocked at speeds greater than 80 miles per hour. Most tornadoes last for only a few minutes, traveling an average of four miles before dissipating.

The swirling winds inside a tornado are so strong that they can easily destroy an ordinary anemometer, the instrument meteorologists use to measure wind speed. At one time, scientists could only estimate tornado wind speed by analyzing films of tornadoes and by viewing the damage and destruction the storms caused. Studies determined that most tornadoes rotate at speeds of 115 to 150 miles per hour, while the strongest tornado winds exceed 250 miles per hour!

WATERSPOUTS

A waterspout is a vortex of air and water located over a large body of water. A waterspout draws water into the air, but it looks like a stream of water pouring out of the base of a cloud.

A *tornadic* waterspout is a tornado that forms over land and then moves over water. A *fair-weather* waterspout forms over water. Fair-weather waterspouts are produced by tall cumulus clouds and small thunderstorms.

Waterspouts generally have wind speeds of less than 50 miles per hour, move more slowly than tornadoes, and last for about 10 minutes. Although waterspouts are usually weaker and smaller than tornadoes, they can still be a danger to boaters. Nearly 100 waterspouts occur each month over the shallow coastal waters of the Florida Keys.

A portable Doppler radar dish

In the past few decades, meteorologists have developed new ways to study tornadoes. With a system called Doppler radar, scientists use radio signals to measure tornado wind speed—at a safe distance from the storm. In the early 1980s, scientists at the government's National Severe Storms Laboratory in Norman, Oklahoma, developed an instrument called TOTO (*TO*table *T*ornado *O*bservatory). TOTO was a sturdy, 400-pound weather station, capable of measuring wind speed, wind direction, and other weather elements and designed to withstand the passage of a tornado. It is no coincidence that the instrument was named after the lovable little dog, Toto, in *The Wizard of Oz*.

During severe thunderstorms, when tornadoes could be expected, a team of courageous meteorologists loaded TOTO into a pickup truck and attempted to place the device in the path of an approaching tornado. Although no tornadoes passed directly over TOTO, several came close.

During the late 1960s, Professor T. Theodore Fujita, a world-famous tornado specialist at the University of Chicago, developed a system for classifying tornadoes based on wind speed and the damage the storms cause. On the Fujita Scale, tornadoes are rated from 0 to 5—"weak" to "violent." Weak tornadoes have wind speeds of less than 112 miles per hour and cause minor damage, such as broken tree branches, torn road signs, and shattered windows. Violent tornadoes have wind speeds of at least 207 miles per hour and are capable of destroying houses and carrying automobiles hundreds of feet through the air.

About 70 percent of all tornadoes reported from 1950 to 1991 were classified as weak, while less than 2 percent were classified as violent. Interestingly enough, the violent tornadoes caused more than two-thirds of all tornado-related deaths.

Predicting when and where tornadoes will form is extremely difficult. Tornadoes and thunderstorms are small-scale weather events, between 100 and 1,000 times smaller than fronts, for instance, which can be hundreds of miles long. Because they are small, tornadoes and thunderstorms often go undetected when they pass between weather observation stations. What's more, meteorologists are still trying to sort out all the factors that cause tornadoes. Scientists don't completely understand why one severe thunderstorm will produce a tornado and another will not.

NEXRAD, or Next Generation Weather Radar, is a system of Doppler radar equipment operated by the National Weather Service.

◄ A NEXRAD station near Denver, Colorado

Tornadoes cut a path as they travel across the land, destroying any trees, buildings, or property they encounter. The long trail of destruction left by a tornado is called a "tornado track."

Typical tornado tracks are about 6 miles long and 500 feet wide. The Tri-State Tornado of 1925 left a track more than 200 miles long, passing through Missouri, Illinois, and Indiana.

◄ Tornado devastation

Despite these obstacles, scientists have many tools that help them forecast tornadoes. At about 1,000 observation stations across the United States, meteorologists monitor ground-level weather conditions around the clock. At each station, weather observers report on thunder, lightning, and cloud types. Sophisticated equipment measures **precipitation** (rain and snow), temperature, humidity, wind speed and direction, and other weather elements.

At more than 100 weather stations, meteorologists release **radiosondes**—weather instruments attached to lighter-than-air balloons—twice each day. Radiosondes measure weather conditions high in the atmosphere and send reports back to Earth via radio signals. Radiosondes help meteorologists learn whether conditions are right for severe thunderstorms and tornadoes to form.

Satellites orbiting hundreds of miles in the air also give forecasters valuable weather information. Satellites carry instruments that measure atmospheric conditions, such as the temperature inside clouds. Photographs taken from satellites help scientists locate thunderstorms and track their movement.

Finally, radar systems provide important information on severe weather. Radar equipment sends out radio signals that bounce off raindrops and hailstones inside clouds. Meteorologists monitor the returning signals to detect and track small thunderstorms that pass between ground-level weather stations.

The advanced Doppler radar system can do everything conventional radar can do and more. Doppler radar can measure winds—including tornado winds—within individual thunderstorm clouds. As more weather stations set up Doppler systems, our ability to forecast tornadoes and severe weather will improve.

Famous Tornadoes

History is rich with reports of the devastating power of tornadoes. A tornado that hit the small town of Barneveld, Wisconsin, on June 8, 1984, leveled 100 homes, killed 9 people, and injured 190 more in just one minute!

The deadliest tornado of all time was the Tri-State Tornado of March 18, 1925. This catastrophic twister claimed the lives of 695 people and injured about 2,000 others. More than 11,000 people lost their homes during the tornado's 3½-hour, 219-mile path of destruction through Missouri, Illinois, and Indiana.

Sometimes a single thunderstorm can produce multiple tornadoes. A "tornado outbreak" consists of multiple tornadoes generated by a long line of thunderstorms, called a squall line. The most violent tornado outbreak in history occurred on April 3 and 4 in 1974. This 16-hour disaster stretched from Mississippi to New York and involved 148 tornadoes raging through 14 states. The outbreak killed more than 300 people, injured 6,000, and caused about $600 million in damage.

Although tornadoes are most common in the central United States, no place is completely protected from the dangers of an occasional tornado. On March 1, 1983, for example, a rare tornado passed through downtown Los Angeles, California. More than 100 homes and businesses were damaged, and 33 people were injured.

A special place in tornado history is reserved for Will Keller, a farmer who lived near Dodge City, Kansas, in the 1920s. Will Keller is the only person known to have viewed the *inside* of a tornado and lived to tell about it! On June 22, 1928, Will hurried his family to the cyclone cellar to escape an approaching tornado. As he looked up at the sky before closing the cellar door, he was astonished to realize that he was looking directly into the center of the tornado's funnel! Will's account of the breathtaking event, told to the National Weather Service office in Dodge City, includes descriptions of strange hissing sounds, small tornadoes forming and breaking away from the larger one, and an eerie glow caused by flashes of lightning.

A funnel cloud descends.

MAKE YOUR OWN TORNADO

You can make your own tornado with two empty plastic soda pop bottles (1 liter, 2 liter, or 16 ounce), two metal bottle caps, some water, and a round balloon. Follow the diagrams below to see how it's done.

1. Take the labels off the pop bottles and fill one bottle about two-thirds full with water.

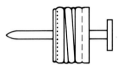

2. Using a nail, punch a hole in the center of each bottle cap. Use a pencil or another sharp object to expand the holes to a width of about ¼ inch. Screw the caps back on the bottles.

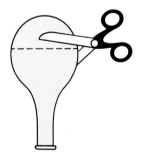

3. Cut the top off a round balloon. Throw the round end away.

4. Fit one end of the remaining part of the balloon over the neck of the empty pop bottle.

5. Flip the empty bottle upside down and fit the other end of the balloon over the neck of the full bottle. The two bottle caps should be as close to one another as possible. Ask a friend to help you make a tight fit.

7. As the water drains, a vortex will appear in the bottle. You've created a tornado!

6. Carefully flip both bottles so that the full bottle is upside down. Hold the bottle necks together tightly with one hand. Using your other hand, shake the top bottle in a circular motion until the water begins to drain through the hole.

3

HURRICANE WEATHER

Hurricanes are fierce rainstorms that form over warm parts of the North Atlantic and the eastern North Pacific oceans. Like tornadoes, hurricanes have a circular shape and intense swirling winds. But, while tornadoes stem from a single thunderstorm, hurricanes are made up of many thunderstorms swirling together.

A typical hurricane is 300 miles across and covers an area of about 70,000 square miles. At the center of the storm we find the **eye**, an area of clear or nearly clear skies with light or calm winds. The eye can be as small as 12 miles across or as large as 125 miles across. It is surrounded by the **eye wall**, a ring of powerful cumulonimbus clouds.

The hurricane was named centuries ago by people living on the islands of the Caribbean Sea, where hurricanes are common. Islanders blamed the devastating storms on Huracan, a god of evil. Hurricanes also form in the western Pacific and Indian oceans, but they often have different names—like "cyclone" in Australia and "typhoon" in India. In parts of Mexico, a hurricane is called *cordonazo*, which means "lash of a whip."

A hurricane smashes into a coastal city.

Hurricanes, like tornadoes, are called "natural disasters"—something people fear and try to avoid. Hurricanes frequently cause death, injury, and billions of dollars in property damage when they smash into populated areas. But hurricanes are a part of life for many people. Where hurricanes are common, people learn to cope with and respect them—much as residents of southern California learn to live with earthquakes. Florida residents are so accustomed to hurricanes that they have even named a college sports team the Miami Hurricanes.

While many people are aware of the damage that hurricanes cause, few people are aware of the benefits. Between 10 and 15 percent of the rain that falls in the southeastern United States comes from hurricanes and other tropical storms. In Mexico and other hurricane-prone countries, farmers rely on hurricanes to bring water to their crops. So, depending on your point of view, hurricanes can be a disaster, a nuisance, or a comfort.

Tropical Weather

Hurricanes originate in the tropics, the regions on Earth near the equator. Tropical weather is different from weather found any-place else on Earth. For one thing, the Earth tilts as it travels around the Sun, causing half of the planet to lean away from the Sun during winter and toward the Sun in summer. The equator, however, never tilts far from the Sun—even in winter. As a result, tropical regions receive a lot of direct sunlight year-round.

In addition, the tropics are covered mostly by oceans. Unlike land, which heats up quickly during the day and cools quickly at night, water warms and cools quite slowly. Even when the Sun goes down at night, tropical oceans stay warm. Temperatures in the tropics are usually quite high—24 hours a day.

Although temperatures in the tropics don't change much from day to night or from season to season, rainfall patterns do change. The dry season in the tropics lasts from late fall to early spring. Late spring to early fall is the wet season, with increased rainfall and cloudiness. The wet season is also hurricane season.

Hurricane Formation

Hurricanes form over tropical oceans when the water at the surface of the sea is particularly warm: 79° F or warmer. The high temperatures cause massive amounts of water to evaporate from the oceans. The evaporation provides the tropical atmosphere with a rich supply of water vapor.

Humid air, or air containing a lot of water vapor, is one crucial ingredient for hurricane formation. Another important hurricane ingredient is **convergence**. Convergence (which means "coming together") occurs when winds blowing from different directions collide with one another—creating a "pileup" of air where they meet. As more wind rushes in, the air at the center of the collision moves upward, becoming an updraft.

Warm ocean waters are the breeding grounds for hurricanes.

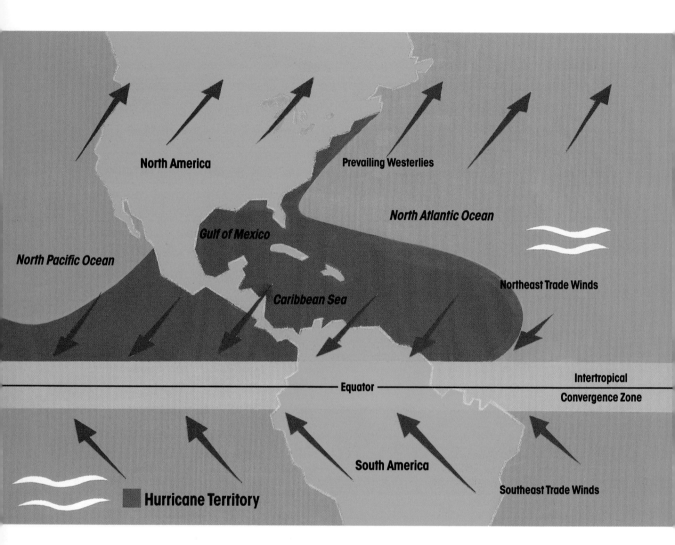

North America

Prevailing Westerlies

North Atlantic Ocean

Gulf of Mexico

North Pacific Ocean

Northeast Trade Winds

Caribbean Sea

Equator

Intertropical
Convergence Zone

South America

Hurricane Territory

Southeast Trade Winds

Convergence commonly occurs near the equator, the meeting place of two powerful wind systems known as the southeast and northeast **trade winds**. Thus, the region near the equator is called the "intertropical convergence zone."

Let's see what happens when we mix the two necessary ingredients of a hurricane: humid air and convergence. First, winds coming from different directions collide and the converging air rises. The rising air (which is rich with water vapor) becomes an updraft, reaches higher altitudes, and quickly cools. The cooling water vapor condenses into an abundance of tiny liquid water droplets, releasing enormous amounts of latent heat into the air.

Does this sound familiar? It should. In Chapter Two, we learned how the condensation process releases latent heat inside thunderstorms. The amount of latent heat released during a tropical thunderstorm, though, is much greater than the amount of latent heat of a thunderstorm found elsewhere on Earth. Because they often form over warm ocean waters, tropical thunderstorms have much more water vapor and much more latent heat than other thunderstorms. As a result, tropical storms are larger, last longer, and bring more rain than thunderstorms in other regions.

At first, convergence and rising air create ordinary thunderstorms in the tropics. As more hot updrafts rise into the storms, the clouds grow larger. Before long, several big thunderstorms might cluster together to create what is called a *tropical disturbance*. A tropical disturbance is the first stage in the formation of a hurricane.

The next stage in the life of a hurricane occurs when the cluster of thunderstorms grows larger and begins to swirl. (Hurricanes and other strong winds swirl because of a complicated phenomenon known as the **Coriolis force**, which is created as the Earth rotates beneath the wind.) The spinning cluster becomes a large vortex, with winds from outside the storm swirling in toward the eye wall.

As the powerful updrafts suck in more and more air, winds swirl in toward the eye wall faster and faster. When the swirling winds reach speeds of 23 miles per hour, the vortex is called a *tropical depression*. When wind speeds reach 40 miles per hour, we call the vortex a *tropical storm*. At 74 miles per hour, we call the storm a *hurricane*.

Hurricane Movement

Like tornadoes, hurricanes travel while they spin—generally moving in predictable ways. Let's follow the path of a typical hurricane that forms just north of the equator in the Atlantic Ocean. Pushed by the northeast trade winds, the hurricane will move from east to west at a speed of 10 to 15 miles per hour. As it approaches the North American mainland, the hurricane will turn north and travel along the coastline.

Hurricane Elena as seen from the space shuttle *Discovery*

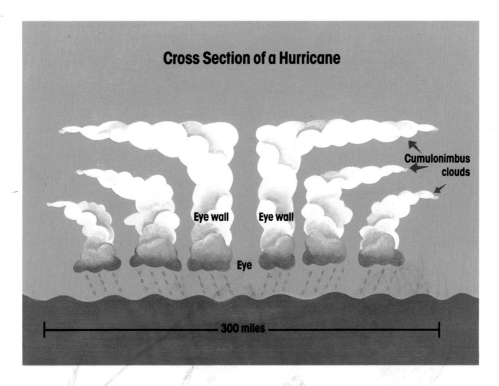

Cross Section of a Hurricane

Cumulonimbus clouds

Eye wall Eye wall

Eye

300 miles

Soon the hurricane will enter the zone of the **prevailing westerlies**, strong winds blowing around the Earth from west to east. Steered by the prevailing westerlies, the storm will head eastward, back out to sea. Because the prevailing westerlies are stronger than the trade winds, the hurricane will move more quickly—perhaps as fast as 50 miles per hour.

Like tornadoes, hurricanes can behave in peculiar ways. In 1963 Hurricane Flora stalled over eastern Cuba for five days before moving on toward the North American coast. Hurricane Betsy followed a haphazard path through the Caribbean Sea before passing into the Gulf of Mexico and striking Louisiana in 1965.

Hurricane damage on the South Carolina coast

Most hurricanes last for five to seven days. The storms dissipate when their energy source—latent heat—is cut off. When a hurricane crosses over land, for instance, or onto the cool ocean water outside the tropics, the storm no longer encounters vast amounts of hot air. Latent heat decreases, and the storm dies out.

Hurricane Andrew did not die out when it hit Florida in 1992, though. The storm moved quickly across the narrow Florida peninsula and then reached the Gulf of Mexico. There, warm waters fed more water vapor into the storm, and Andrew picked up speed. The hurricane crashed into the coast of Louisiana, where it finally lost strength.

As a hurricane dissipates, it passes through its earlier stages in reverse order—going from tropical storm to tropical depression to tropical disturbance—before fizzling out altogether. These lesser storms are significant in themselves, however. They can still bring strong winds and heavy precipitation.

One fascinating hurricane feature is that after reaching land, the large cumulonimbus clouds of a hurricane often generate tornadoes. Suppose you survived a passing hurricane. The last thing you would need to add to your troubles would be a tornado! This is one case where the expression "When it rains, it pours" rings true.

4

HURRICANES AND PEOPLE

If a hurricane were to pass directly over you, you would experience vigorous winds, heavy precipitation (in the form of rain and hail), and frequent lightning. The weather would grow worse as the storm approached. The strongest winds would blow at the eye wall. When the eye wall passed, you would be standing in the eye of the hurricane.

The clearing skies and light winds of the hurricane's eye have fooled many people into thinking that a storm has passed them by. These people were unpleasantly surprised when the storm resumed— with (because hurricane winds blow in a circle) violent winds coming from the opposite direction!

Hurricane winds are not usually as strong as tornado winds. But since hurricanes are thousands of times larger than tornadoes and last for days rather than just minutes, hurricanes have more room and more time to work their damage. When a hurricane reaches land, it is not uncommon for the storm to uproot trees and hurl buildings through the air. When Hurricane Frederic slammed into the Gulf Coast of Mississippi and Alabama in 1979, the storm's 132

At the Hurricane Hugo Help Center, civil defense workers assist people who have lost homes and property during the destructive storm.

mile-per-hour winds killed five people, destroyed hundreds of buildings, and caused $2.3 billion in damage.

But rainfall can be even more destructive than wind during a hurricane. The average daily rainfall from a passing hurricane is 5 to 10 inches. But the largest storms have been known to dump up to 24 inches of rain in a single day!

Hurricane rainfall can flood low-lying coastal regions all by itself. But hurricanes also cause a **storm surge**, an abnormal rise in ocean levels—often by 10 feet or more. A storm surge occurs when driving winds at sea pile up water along the coast. When the swell of water finally pours in over land, it damages everything in its path, often causing injuries and death.

Many people build vacation homes in hurricane-prone areas—at their own risk!

The storm surge created by Hurricane Camille as it smashed into the Mississippi coastline in 1969 was a whopping 23 feet above the normal high-tide water level. The flooding (along with Camille's 184 mile-per-hour winds) destroyed thousands of buildings and claimed more than 200 lives.

Studying Hurricanes

As with tornadoes, much remains to be learned about why, when, where, and how hurricanes form. In addition to trying to predict hurricane formation, meteorologists also focus on tracking *existing* hurricanes and tropical storms. The safety of people in hurricane-prone regions depends on accurate forecasts of hurricane movement. People in the path of a hurricane need advance warning to be able to evacuate their homes.

Unless you happen to be in a spacecraft orbiting the Earth, it is impossible to observe an entire hurricane at once. Much of what meteorologists know about hurricanes comes from photographs taken by satellites. Scientists use these pictures to identify where and when tropical storms and hurricanes form, to track their movement, and to estimate their strength.

As useful as satellite photos are, they can't provide some critical information—like wind speed measurements. Doppler radar *could* measure hurricane wind speed, but hurricanes are often located far out to sea, well beyond the reach of any radar system.

Because of the limitations of satellite photography and radar, meteorologists who study hurricanes have to go right to the source—"right to the eye of the storm," you might say. The government's National Hurricane Center in Coral Gables, Florida, operates airplanes that are specially designed to fly through hurricanes. Talk about a bumpy ride!

Radar systems tracked Hurricane Hugo as it neared the North American coast. The most violent areas of the storm are shown in red. The black area at the center is eye of the hurricane.

Daring pilots and meteorologists regularly fly "weather reconnaissance (exploration) missions" to measure weather conditions *inside* hurricanes. In addition to measuring air pressure, temperature, humidity, and wind speed and direction at flight-level, the flight crew measures weather conditions at the ocean surface by releasing **dropwinsondes** from the aircraft. Dropwinsondes are miniature weather stations similar to radiosondes. But rather than floating upward with a balloon, dropwinsondes are attached to a parachute and fall slowly toward the ocean.

Using satellite photographs, measurements from weather reconnaissance aircraft, and readings from other sources—such as commercial airplanes or ships at sea—meteorologists try to predict where a particular hurricane will move in the coming 48 hours. Powerful computers help the scientists analyze the information and prepare the forecast.

If scientists believe a storm poses a direct threat to an inhabited area, the National Hurricane Center will issue a hurricane *watch* for the region. If a storm is likely to strike within 24 hours, a hurricane *warning* will be issued.

If a hurricane watch is issued for your area, stay tuned to a battery-operated radio or television. During a hurricane warning, local civil defense authorities might instruct you to evacuate your home. To prepare for the onslaught of fierce winds and driving rains, many coastal residents board up the windows of their houses and businesses before a hurricane.

Hurricane watches and warnings have saved countless lives. As Hurricane Allen roared onshore along the south Texas coast on August 10, 1980, few local residents were on hand to greet the killer

HURRICANE ENERGY

The massive amounts of water vapor that condense in the tropics give hurricanes a lot of latent heat energy. In fact, the energy generated daily by a hurricane is about 200 times greater than the total electrical energy produced in the United States each day!

Along with the latent heat energy come vast amounts of rain. Between 10 and 20 billion tons of water fall from a typical hurricane in a single day.

Ocean waters swell as a hurricane approaches land.

storm. Because the National Hurricane Center had issued warnings, more than 200,000 people had fled the area many hours in advance.

A few days earlier, Allen, which brought 170 mile-per-hour winds and extensive flooding, had killed nearly 300 people in the Yucatán Peninsula of Mexico. Those unfortunate people did not have the benefit of an advance warning system.

Hurricane Names

I'm sure you've noticed by now that all hurricanes are given human names. This wasn't always the case, however. Prior to the 1940s, hurricanes were identified by their location. They were labeled according to latitude and longitude numbers found on a map. During World War II, scientists began labeling hurricanes with radio code words such as Able and Baker. In 1953 the

Pacific Hurricane Rita

National Weather Service began using female names to identify hurricanes. The names were assigned in alphabetical order each year. The year's first storm name began with the letter A, the second with the letter B, and so on.

Since 1979, hurricanes have been assigned male as well as female names. If you were a comedian, you could call 1979 the "year of the *him*micane." Each year hurricane names alternate from male to female in alphabetical order. Separate lists are created for Atlantic and eastern Pacific hurricanes. The first five Atlantic hurricanes of 1992 were named Andrew, Bonnie, Charley, Danielle, and Earl.

Famous Hurricanes

Although hurricanes can be catastrophic, they are not uncommon events. On average, four or five hurricanes form in the Atlantic Ocean every year. Three or more tropical storms that don't reach hurricane intensity (winds of 74 miles per hour) also occur yearly.

Throughout history, a few hurricanes stand out. One such storm occurred 250 years ago. On October 22, 1743, the early American statesman and meteorologist Benjamin Franklin was looking forward to enjoying the rare spectacle of a total lunar eclipse. His plans were thwarted when a tropical cyclone filled the skies over Philadelphia with violent storm clouds.

After corresponding with his brother in Boston, Franklin was surprised to learn that the cyclone had been there too. He correctly reasoned that the storm had traveled between the two coastal cities. Franklin's realization that storms can travel great distances was an early milestone in the science of meteorology.

Deadly hurricanes have plagued coastal residents since prehistory. In 1893 about 1,000 people in Charleston, South Carolina, and 2,000 people in Louisiana perished as hurricanes ripped through the Atlantic and Gulf Coast regions. The Gulf Coast hurricane of 1900 caused a storm surge of 30 feet that demolished Galveston, Texas, and killed more than 5,000 people. The worst storm in modern history was the cyclone that struck the Asian nation of Bangladesh in 1970, taking the lives of more than 300,000 people. Bangladesh was struck by another killer cyclone in 1991. The storm created a 20-foot tidal wave that claimed the lives of 140,000 people, killed a million cattle, and destroyed more than a million homes.

More and more people are moving to coastal areas in the southeastern United States, ignoring the dangers of hurricanes and building expensive homes and businesses. As a result, property damage caused by hurricanes has increased steadily in recent years.

When Hurricane Hugo slammed into the coast of South Carolina in 1989, for instance, the storm caused $7 billion in damage. Hugo destroyed beachfront homes and buildings and wiped out about $1 billion worth of timber when it toppled more than one-third of the trees in South Carolina's forests.

Hurricane Andrew was one of the most destructive hurricanes ever to hit the United States. The storm devastated southern Florida near Homestead on August 24, 1992, and smashed into the Louisiana coast two days later.

More than a million people evacuated their homes as Andrew approached. Wind speeds peaked at 165 miles per hour during the hurricane, and ocean levels surged more than 10 feet above the normal mark.

Residents of Kendall, Florida, return after Hurricane Andrew to find rubble where their house once stood.

Andrew caused $20 billion worth of damage in Florida and $300 million in Louisiana. The storm reduced hundreds of square miles to rubble and left almost 300,000 people homeless. After the hurricane, the United States military set up tent shelters and provided medical care and food to Andrew's victims.

In spite of the population increase in areas visited by tropical cyclones, the hurricane-related death toll continues to decrease—thanks to the success of the hurricane watch and warning system, and to civil defense authorities who make evacuation plans for coastal

After a hurricane or tornado has passed, the work of cleaning up and repairing the damage begins.

residents. Because of advance warning, Andrew, the costliest hurricane of all time, claimed the lives of fewer than 30 people. As meteorologists continue to make improvements in hurricane observation and forecasting, the death toll should decrease even further.

By now you have come to understand and respect the spectacular phenomena of tornadoes and hurricanes. In some ways, tornadoes and hurricanes are similar. Both are violent atmospheric vortexes, and both are closely involved with thunderstorms. But tornadoes and hurricanes are also very different. Tornadoes form over land and hurricanes form at sea. Tornadoes are several thousand times smaller than hurricanes.

The early American settlers didn't always recognize these differences, however. In the United States, a number of places far from the sea have names like "Hurricane Hollows" and "Hurricane Mountains." No doubt, fierce storms have visited these places. But the early settlers apparently didn't know that hurricanes die out once they reach land. The weather events mentioned in the place names were probably tornadoes.

While the disadvantages of tornadoes and hurricanes are tremendous, the benefits of these storms are also quite significant, especially for farmers. Much of the rain in the Tornado Alley region of the central United States falls from severe thunderstorms. Hurricanes contribute a substantial portion of the rainfall in coastal regions.

Tornadoes and hurricanes, with all their destruction, remind us of the incredible power of the forces of nature. The coming years will yield new discoveries that will help us better understand the greatest storms on Earth.

Hurricane Kamysi in the Indian Ocean near Madagascar

GLOSSARY

condensation: the process by which water vapor cools and changes into liquid water

convection: the rising motion of warm air

convergence: the meeting of winds blowing from different directions

Coriolis force: a force, created by the Earth's rotation, that causes winds to curve

cumulonimbus cloud: a massive cloud that produces rain, hail, thunder, and lightning.

cumulus cloud: a puffy white cloud with rounded sides and a flat base

downdraft: a downward moving current of air

dropwinsonde: a package of meteorological instruments that is attached to a parachute and dropped from an airplane

evaporate: to change from liquid into gas by heating

eye: the calm area in the center of a hurricane

eye wall: a ring of cumulonimbus clouds surrounding the eye of a hurricane

front: a boundary between warm and cold air

frontal lifting: the rising motion of warm air over cold air at a front

funnel cloud: the twisting cloud that precedes a tornado

humidity: the amount of water vapor in the air

hurricane: a violent tropical storm made up of a swirling cluster of thunderstorm clouds

latent heat: heat that turns water into water vapor. Latent heat is also released as water vapor condenses.

mammatus clouds: bulging, pouchlike clouds that hang down from the underside of a cumulonimbus cloud

orographic lifting: the rising motion of wind as it climbs the slope of a mountain

precipitation: any kind of rain or snow, including freezing rain and hail

prevailing westerlies: powerful wind belts found in the middle latitudes that blow around the Earth from west to east

radar: as used in weather forecasting, radio signals that bounce off raindrops and snowflakes

radiosonde: a package of meteorological instruments that is attached to a balloon and released into the atmosphere

satellite: a vehicle that orbits the Earth, taking photographs and readings of atmospheric conditions

storm surge: a swell of sea water, created by a hurricane, which often floods coastal areas

thunderstorm: a fierce rainstorm often accompanied by lightning and thunder

tornado: a violent windstorm that takes the shape of a funnel

trade winds: great wind belts, just north and south of the equator, that blow around the Earth from east to west

updrafts: upward moving currents of air

vortex: a swirling mass of fluid, such as air

water vapor: water in gas form

wind shear: different wind speed or direction at different altitudes

wall cloud: a large rotating section at the base of a thunderstorm cloud

METRIC CONVERSION CHART		
When you know:	**multiply by:**	**to find:**
acres	.41	hectares
square miles	2.59	square kilometers
gallons	3.79	liters
inches	2.54	centimeters
feet	.30	meters
yards	.91	meters
miles	1.61	kilometers
pounds	.45	kilograms
tons	.91	metric tons
degrees Fahrenheit	.56 (after subtracting 32)	degrees Celsius

INDEX

ACKNOWLEDGMENTS

Photographs and illustrations used with permission of National Center for Atmospheric Research, pp: 2, 7, 20 (top and bottom), 28, 30 (top), 64; National Weather Service, p. 9; Michael Mogil, pp. 10, 15, 56 (bottom); Utah DWR, p. 11; Tom Dietrich, p. 13; National Oceanic and Atmospheric Administration, pp. 14, 27; Liz Monson, pp. 17, 24, 40, 43; West Publishing Company, p. 19; Visuals Unlimited, pp. 21, 37, 48 (Science VU), p. 30 bottom (Albert Copley), p. 33 (Patricia Armstrong), p. 51 (Kjell B. Sandved), p. 52 (Robert F. Meyers); Lucy Sukalo, pp. 23, 56 (top); Laura Westlund, pp. 34, 35; Steve Johnson, p. 39; National Aeronautics and Space Administration, pp. 42, 58; Jay Browne, South Carolina Forestry Commission, pp. 44, 49; County of Charleston, p. 47; Jim Virga, The Sun-Sentinel, p. 55. Cover photograph: Visuals Unlimited (Kjell B. Sandved).